Faber Studio Collection

Selections from PreTime® Piano

Arranged by Nancy and Randall Faber

This book belongs to: _____

Popular

Classics

Jazz & Blues

Rock 'n Roll

and more...

Production Coordinator: Jon Ophoff
Design and Illustration: Terpstra Design, San Francisco
Engraving: Dovetree Productions, Inc.

FABER
PIANO ADVENTURES®
3042 Creek Drive
Ann Arbor, Michigan 48108

A NOTE TO TEACHERS

The **Faber Studio Collections** offer a mix of styles with selections from the *PreTime®* to *BigTime®* Piano Supplementary Library. This sampling from the *Popular*, *Classics*, *Jazz & Blues*, *Rock 'n Roll*, and other favorite books presents an array of genres at each level. When a style resonates, the student can pick up just the right book for follow-up.

The **PreTime® Studio Collection** is not only appealing to the beginning piano student, but is especially formulated for the piano teacher. The selections provide excellent reinforcement of basic rhythms and note reading. Teacher duets for each piece provide vitality, color, and ensemble experience!

This book is part of the *PreTime® Piano* series arranged by Faber and Faber. "PreTime" designates the Primer Level of the *PreTime® to BigTime® Piano Supplementary Library*.

Following are the levels of the supplementary library, which lead from *PreTime®* to *BigTime®*.

PreTime® Piano	(Primer Level)
PlayTime® Piano	(Level 1)
ShowTime® Piano	(Level 2A)
ChordTime® Piano	(Level 2B)
FunTime® Piano	(Level 3A-3B)
BigTime® Piano	(Level 4-above)

Each level offers books in a variety of styles, making it possible for the teacher to offer stimulating material for every student. For a complimentary detailed listing, e-mail faber@pianoadventures.com or write us at the mailing address below.

Visit **www.PianoAdventures.com.**

ONLINE SUPPORT

Visit **www.PianoAdventures.com/studio** to find online support for this book!

ISBN 978-1-61677-640-4

TABLE OF CONTENTS

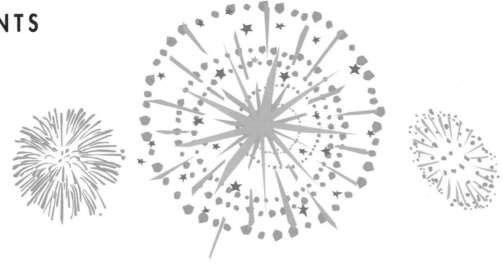

When Can I See You Again?

from Walt Disney's *WRECK-IT RALPH*

Words and Music by
ADAM YOUNG, MATTHEW THIESSEN
and BRIAN LEE

Fast

It's been fun, but now I've got to go.

Life is way too short to take it slow. But be -

Teacher Duet: (Student plays 1 octave higher)

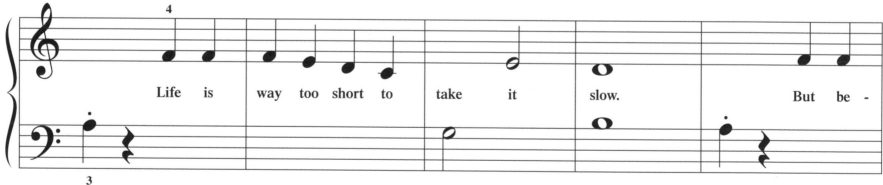

FF3016

Classics

A Little Night Music

from *Eine Kleine Nachtmusik*

WOLFGANG AMADEUS MOZART

Quickly, with energy

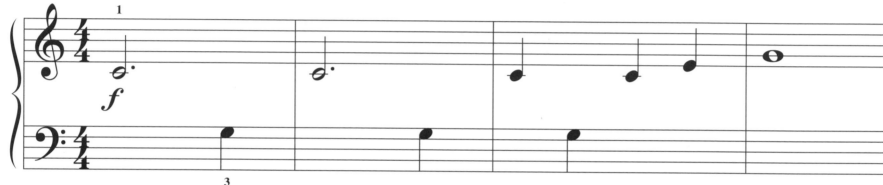

Teacher Duet: (Student plays 2 octaves higher)

FF3016

Hard Rock Candy

Music by NANCY & RANDALL FABER
Lyrics by CRYSTAL BOWMAN

Moderately

Clear and sweet, my fa - v'rite treat is hard rock can - dy.

Some for you and some for me, it sure is dan - dy.

Teacher Duet: (Student plays 1 octave higher)

FF3016

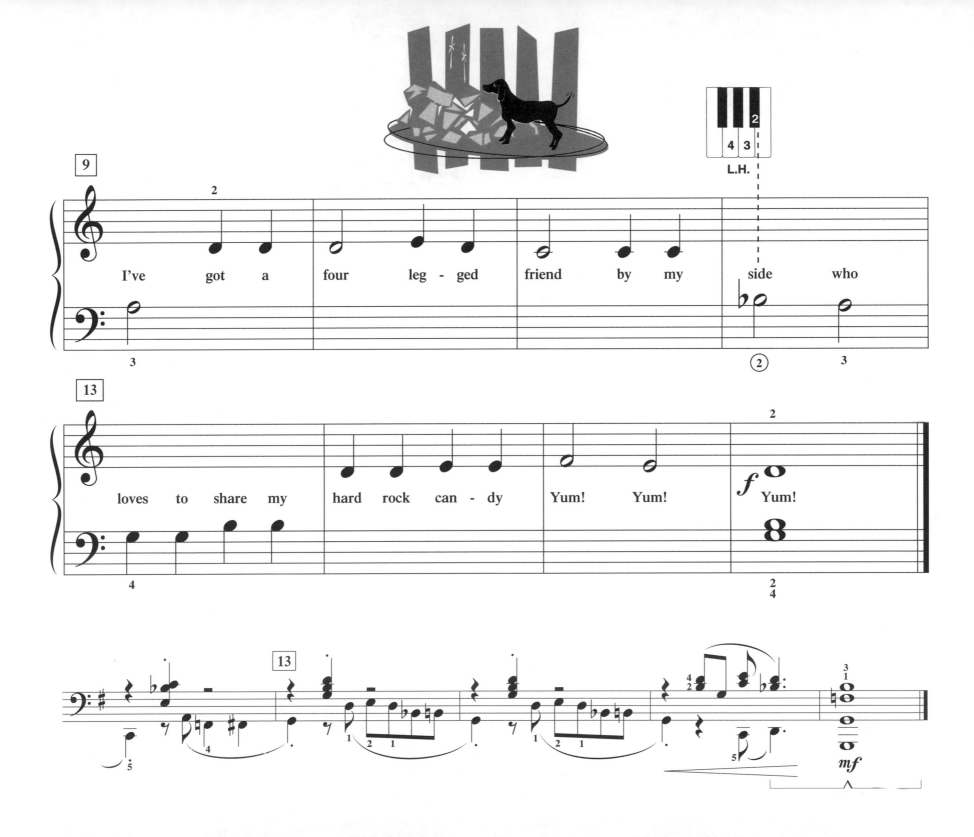

Hound Dog Blues

Music by NANCY FABER
Lyrics by CRYSTAL BOWMAN

With big sad eyes

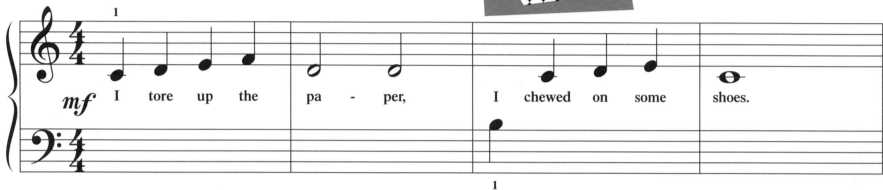

I tore up the pa - per, I chewed on some shoes.

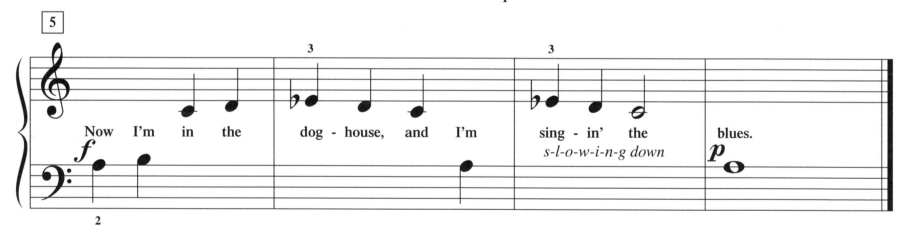

Now I'm in the dog - house, and I'm sing - in' the blues.
s-l-o-w-i-n-g down

Teacher Duet: (Student plays 1 octave higher)

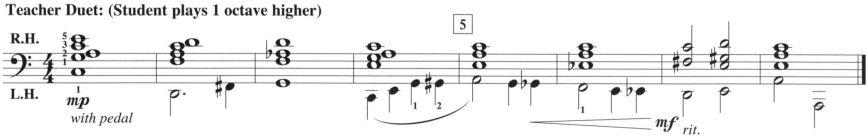

FF3016

Row, Row, Row Your Boat

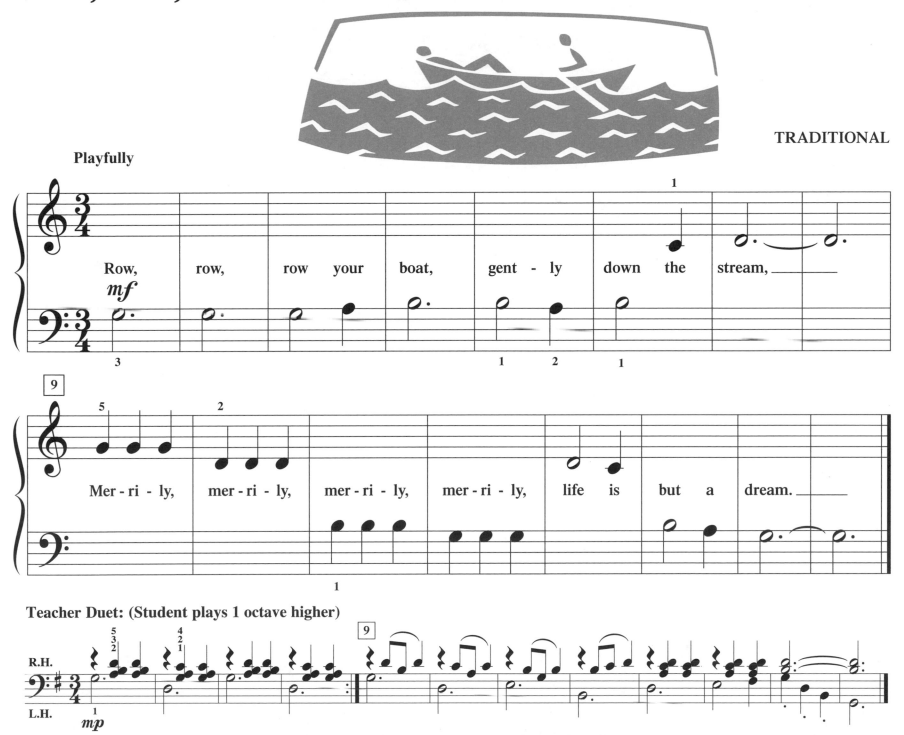

TRADITIONAL

Teacher Duet: (Student plays 1 octave higher)

Part of Your World

from Walt Disney's *THE LITTLE MERMAID*

Music by ALAN MENKEN
Lyrics by HOWARD ASHMAN

Moderately

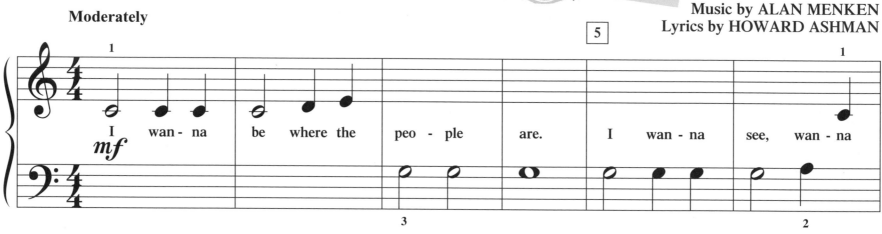

I wan - na be where the peo - ple are. I wan - na see, wan - na

see 'em dan - cin', walk - in' a - round on those what d'ya call 'em

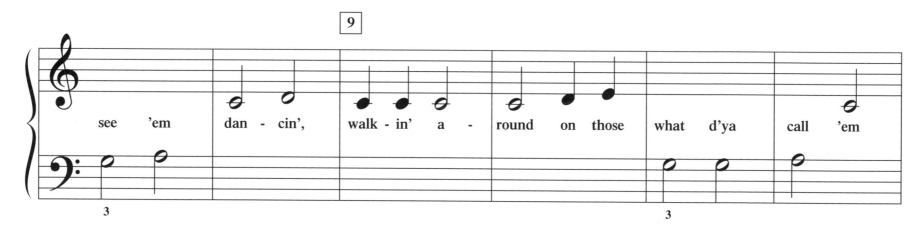

Teacher Duet: (Student plays 1 octave higher)

R.H.

L.H. *with pedal*
mp

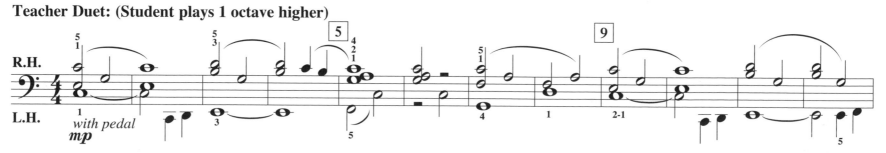

FF3016

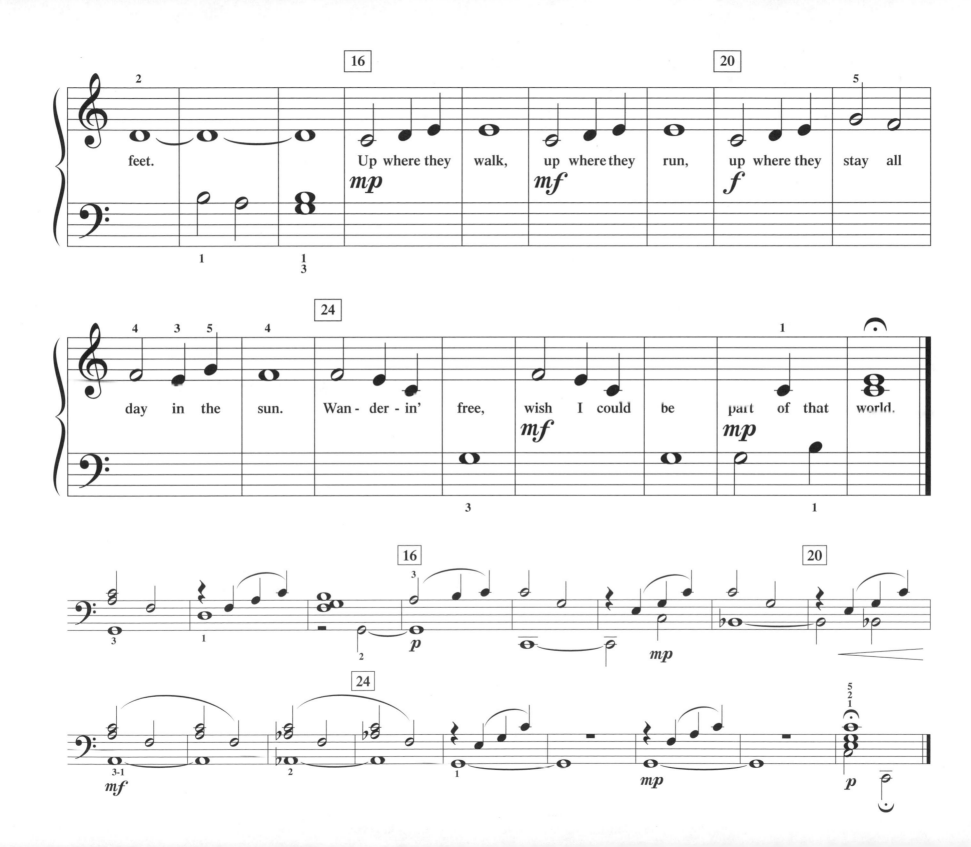

I've Got the Joy, Joy, Joy

Notice the R.H. starting finger!

Lively

TRADITIONAL

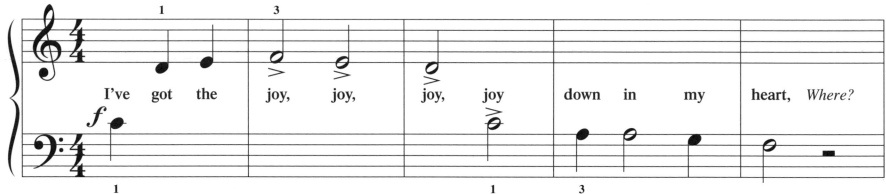

I've got the joy, joy, joy, joy down in my heart, *Where?*

Down in my heart, *Where?* Down in my heart. I've got the

Teacher Duet: (Student plays 1 octave higher)

FF3016

On Top of Spaghetti

Words and Music by
TOM GLAZER

Moderately fast, with spirit

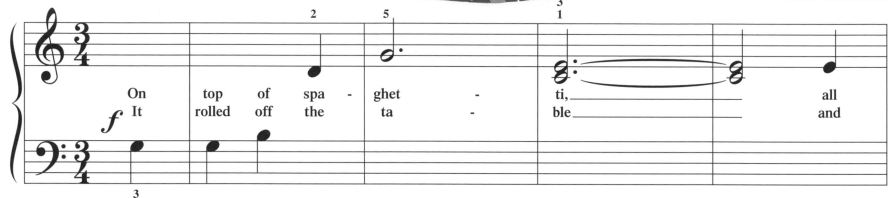

On top of spa - ghet - ti,_____ all
It rolled off the ta - ble_____ and

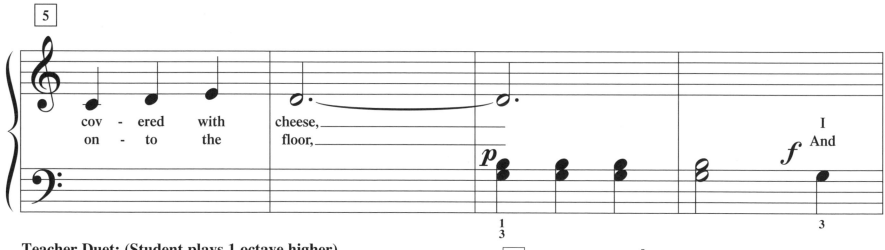

cov - ered with cheese,_____ I
on - to the floor,_____ And

Teacher Duet: (Student plays 1 octave higher)

R.H.

L.H.

FF3016

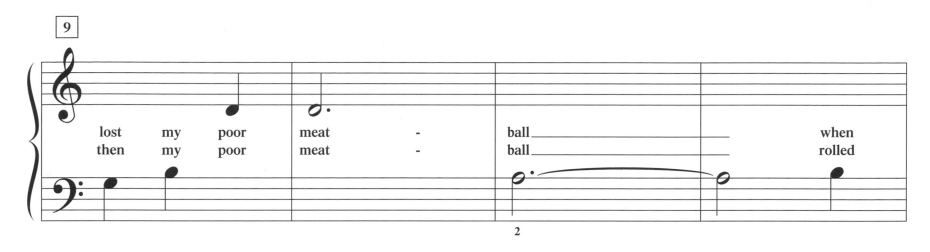

lost my poor meat - ball when
then my poor meat - ball rolled

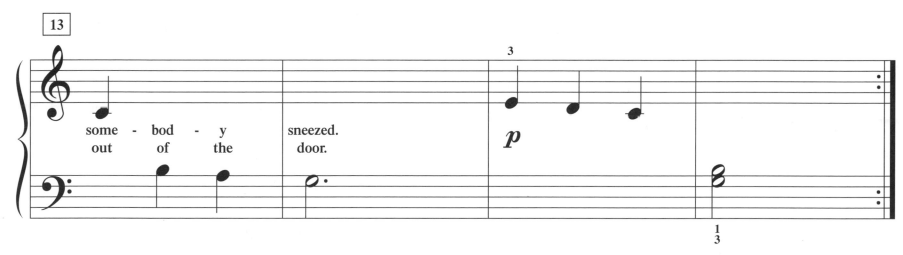

some - bod - y sneezed.
out of the door.

p

2. It rolled in the garden and under a bush,
 And then my poor meatball was nothing but mush.
 The mush was as tasty as tasty could be,
 And early next summer, it grew into a tree.

3. The tree was covered with beautiful moss;
 It grew lovely meatball and tomato sauce.
 So if you eat spaghetti all covered with cheese,
 Hold onto your meatballs and don't ever sneeze.

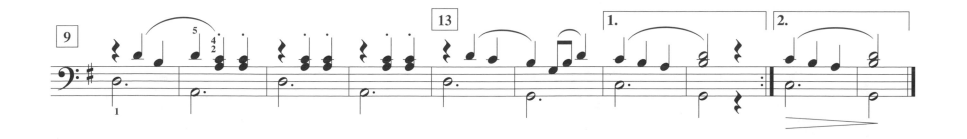

Jazz Man

Music by NANCY FABER
Lyrics by CRYSTAL BOWMAN

With energy

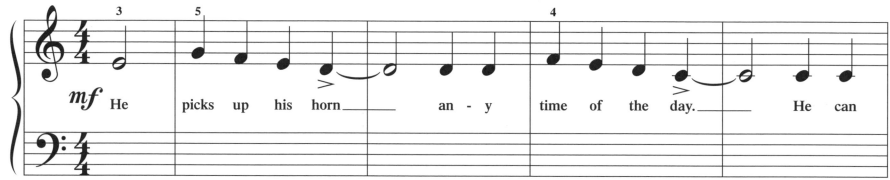

mf He picks up his horn ___ an - y time of the day. ___ He can

play an - y tune ___ that you ask him to play. ___ He's

Teacher Duet: (Student plays 1 octave higher)

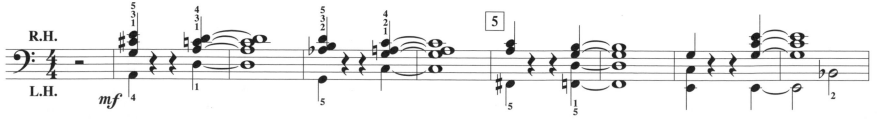

FF3016

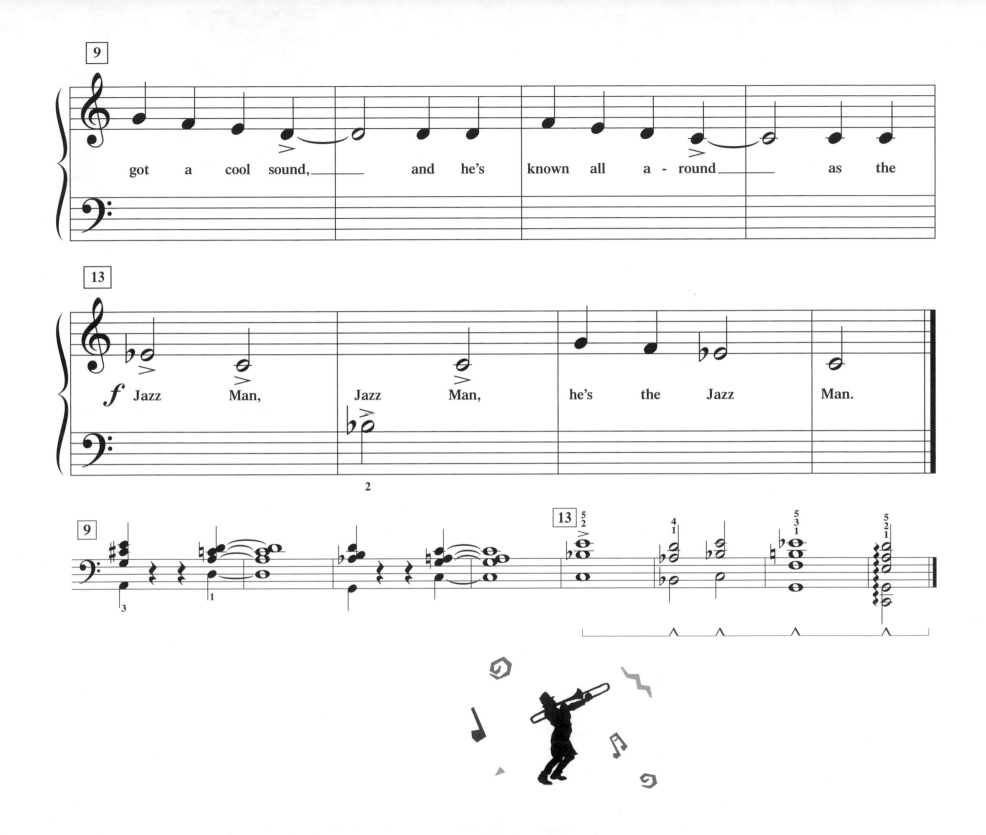

Hush, Little Baby

Gently

TRADITIONAL

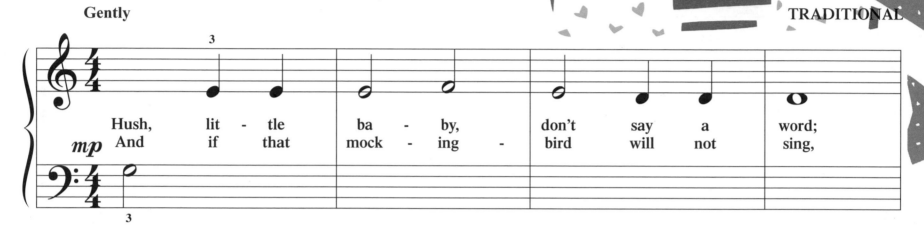

Hush, lit - tle ba - by, don't say a word;
And if that mock - ing - bird will not sing,

Dad - dy's gon - na buy you a mock - ing - bird.
Dad - dy's gon - na buy you a dia - mond ring.

Teacher Duet: (Student plays 1 octave higher)

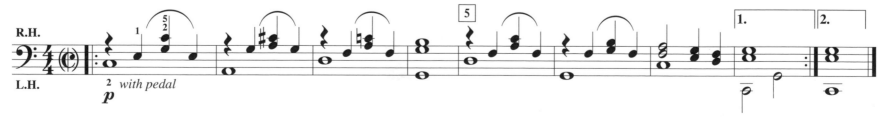

R.H.

L.H.   *with pedal*
p

FF3016